AMERICAN LEGENDS™

Annie Oakley

Frances E. Ruffin

The Rosen Publishing Group's

PowerKids Press™

New York

For my brother David, who has always been there for me

Grateful acknowledgment is made for the biographical information about Annie Oakley that was given by Bess Edwards of the Annie Oakley Foundation, P.O. Box 127, Greenville, OH 45331.

Published in 2002 by The Rosen Publishing Group, Inc.
29 East 21st Street, New York, NY 10010

First Edition

Book Design: Michael de Guzman

Project Editor: Kathy Campbell

Photo Credits: pp. 4, 11, 16, 19 © The Granger Collection; pp. 7, 12 © Bettmann/CORBIS; p. 8 © Michael Masalan Historic Photographs/CORBIS; p. 15 © Buffalo Bill Historical Center, Cody, WY; p. 20 © CORBIS.

Ruffin, Frances E.
    Annie Oakley / Frances E. Ruffin.— 1st ed.
        p. cm. — (American legends)
Includes index.
    ISBN 0-8239-5824-8 (lib. bdg.)
    1. Oakley, Annie, 1860–1926—Juvenile literature. 2. Shooters of firearms—United States—Biography—Juvenile literature. 3. Women entertainers—United States—Biography—Juvenile literature. 4. Frontier and pioneer life—West (U.S.)—Juvenile literature. [1. Oakley, Annie, 1860–1926. 2. Sharpshooters. 3. Entertainers. 4. Women—Biography.]
    I. Title. II. American legends (New York, N.Y.)
    GV1157.O3 R84 2002
    799.3'092—dc21
                                                                    00-012147

Manufactured in the United States of America

Contents

As an adult, Annie Oakley stood only 5 feet (1.5 m) tall and weighed just 100 pounds (45.4 kg). She is seen in this picture wearing some of the medals she won on tour. She even performed before Queen Victoria of England and other world leaders.

Annie Oakley

At the end of the nineteenth century, Annie Oakley was the most famous **markswoman** in the United States. She was one of the best **sharpshooters** in the world. When Annie took aim with her rifle and fired, she never missed her target. Being able to shoot well was important during Annie's time. People used guns for hunting food and for protection. Her skills with a gun were so exact that Sitting Bull, the **Sioux** chief, called her Little Sure Shot in 1884. Annie first used her gun to survive. Then she used it to entertain people. As the star of a popular Wild West show, she drew crowds whenever she appeared onstage. Annie's ability to shoot straight, her faith in herself, and her **determination** made her a **legend**.

What Is a Legend?

There have been books, plays, and movies about Annie Oakley's life. The stories about Annie Oakley have become legends. Many of these stories were true and actually happened. Like some stories about famous people, they may have been **exaggerated** in some way. One story told that Annie's hair turned white only 17 hours after she was involved in a train wreck in 1901. This story is untrue. Annie Oakley, who was born in Ohio, became a **symbol** of the western part of the United States. Annie had never traveled west of the Mississippi River, though, until she was 24 years old. More than 100 years later, Annie Oakley still helps us to enjoy the images and legends that people have about America's Wild West.

One of Annie's special feats was using a mirror to shoot at a target that was behind her. This special act, called a stunt, required great sharpshooting skills.

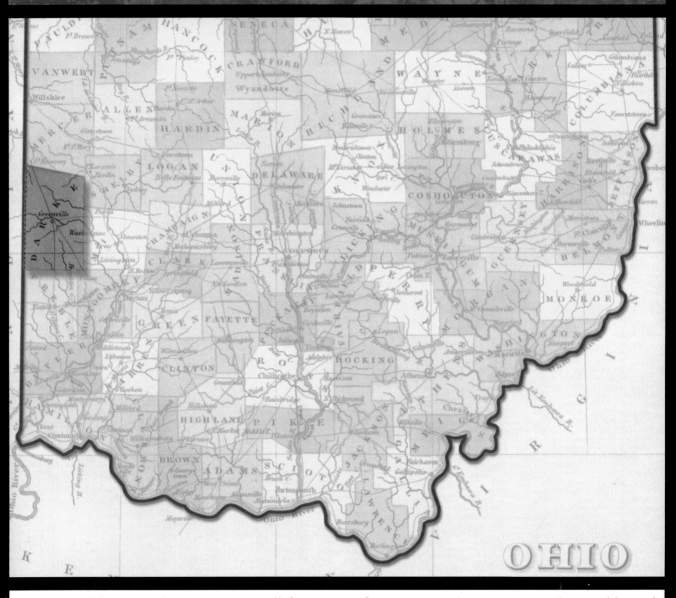

OHIO

Annie Oakley was born on a small farm in a forest in Darke County, Ohio. Although her fame and travels took her far away from Darke County, Annie always came back to Darke County to visit her relatives and friends who lived there.

Born in a Log Cabin

Annie Oakley's real name was Phoebe Ann Mozee, but everyone called her Annie. She was born on August 13, 1860, in Darke County, Ohio. She was the sixth daughter of Jacob and Susan Mozee, who were **Quakers**. A fire had destroyed the family's home and business in Pennsylvania in 1855. This forced the family to move to a small farm in Darke County, Ohio. The farm was surrounded by wilderness. Jacob built the one-room log cabin in which the family lived. Three more children were born after Annie, including her brother, John. Her family was poor. Jacob fed his family with **game** that he shot or trapped in the woods. Young Annie and John trailed after their father. Annie loved the animals and the plants that she found in the nearby forest.

Tragedy Strikes a Family

By the time Annie was six years old, her father and older sister had died, leaving the family in **debt**. Annie's mother had to sell the farm and move the family to a rented farm. As Susan Mozee struggled to pay off her debts, Annie decided she could help her mother. Her brother John used their father's rifle to shoot game to feed the family. Annie once begged John to let her try to fire the gun. She aimed and shot a rabbit on her very first try. At age ten, Annie was sent to live with her mother's friends who were in charge of the Darke County Infirmary. People who were ill or old lived there. Children who were orphans lived there, too. During the late 1800s, children of poor families sometimes had to live and work away from home to help support their families.

Annie learned to shoot a gun when she was ten years old. After her father died, Annie hunted for game to put food on the table. Annie poses here (center) with one of her sharpshooting rifles. She is taking aim at targets (left and right).

Annie hunted to earn a living, but she liked to enter shooting contests to show off her skills. In her later years, Annie wrote that "After the age of ten, I never had a nickel in my pocket that I didn't earn."

Annie Starts a Business

In 1875, Annie was 15 years old. She had earned the honor of being the best sharpshooter in Darke County. By then, she had left the infirmary and returned to her family's home. She also had started her own business. The woods around the farm were full of small game and birds, such as pheasants and quails. Annie shot and sold her fresh game to a local grocer. The grocer sold the extra meat to big restaurants and hotels in Cincinnati, Ohio. This big city was about 80 miles (129 km) from Greenville, Ohio. Her business soon became so **prosperous** that she was able to pay off the debts on her mother's home. It was clear that Annie enjoyed shooting a gun because she was good at it.

Meeting Frank Butler

After the Civil War, which ended in 1865, people still enjoyed watching shooting contests. Annie entered these shooting matches and she always won. She competed against men who grew tired of losing to her. They refused to let her enter any more contests. In the spring of 1881, Annie was visiting a small town near Greenville, when she was invited to try her luck in a shooting match. She would compete against a **professional** sharpshooter named Frank Butler. He was one of the three most famous marksmen of that time. Annie entered the contest and won. After her shooting match with Frank Butler, Annie left town with two things: the $50 that she had won and Frank Butler's heart. Annie admired Frank, too. The couple married in June 1882.

This is a photograph of Frank Butler in his later years. Butler did not mind that he lost to a woman shooter when he competed against Annie for the first time. He had fallen in love with her. Annie had thick, brown hair and blue-gray eyes.

Annie Oakley (at top) is seen here with Native Americans in a photograph that shows them in the mountains, possibly in the West. In 1884, Chief Sitting Bull saw Annie perform her act in St. Paul, Minnesota, and adopted her as his daughter.

Taking Her Act on the Road

Beginning in 1882, the couple traveled around the country in a sharpshooting act called Butler and Oakley. Annie had changed her name to Oakley because she liked that name. Another member of the act was their poodle, George. George would sit on a stool with an apple on his head as Annie or Frank shot and split the apple with a bullet. In 1884, while performing in St. Paul, Minnesota, Annie met Sitting Bull, the Sioux chief. Sitting Bull, with other Native American leaders and warriors, had defeated Lieutenant Colonel George Custer and his troops in the Battle of Little Bighorn in 1876. Sitting Bull was so impressed with Annie's talent that he "adopted" her. He named her Watanya Cecilla, which in Sioux means Little Sure Shot.

Star of the Wild West

In 1885, William Cody, who was known as Buffalo Bill, invited Annie to join his traveling show. Cody had been a **pony express** rider, soldier, and hunter. He was a true symbol of the American West. His show, Buffalo Bill's Wild West, featured cowboys, sharpshooters, and Native American performers. Tickets sold out when Annie, known as "the little girl of the Western Plains," appeared. Annie's husband, Frank, became her business manager and stage assistant. People were excited by her **stunts**. She shot equally well with her right or her left hand. She shot a cigarette from Frank's mouth, hit a target behind her by using a mirror, shattered glass balls tossed into the air, and did many other amazing stunts. Her audiences stood and cheered at the end of her act.

This 1901 poster of Annie shows her doing her acts in the show Buffalo Bill's Wild West. She also is shooting a deer in the woods and hunting quail. After performing her act, Annie always gave a girlish skip and a kick before running offstage.

Buffalo Bill's Wild West, seen here in one of their acts, traveled throughout the United States and Europe. People around the world wanted to know what life was like in the American West.

The World's Most Famous Woman

Buffalo Bill's Wild West was so popular that it traveled around the United States and Great Britain, and even toured countries in Europe. Annie performed for Queen Victoria of England in 1887. For many years, Annie Oakley was the most famous woman in the world. When Thomas Edison invented the movie camera, he had Annie do her act in 1894 for some of the first movies ever made. They lasted about 90 seconds. In 1901, a freight train crashed into the train that was carrying Annie and the Wild West performers in Danville, Virginia. Annie was seriously hurt and she had to leave the show. Luckily, she recovered. In 1911, Annie joined a new show called the Young Buffalo's Wild West.

Generous to the End

As Annie grew older, she gave free shooting lessons to women who wanted to become sports shooters and to learn to defend themselves. She taught thousands of women about guns and gun safety. During World War I in 1917, Annie offered to train a **regiment** of women volunteers to fight in the war for the United States. The offer was never accepted. Early in 1926, both Annie and Frank became ill. Annie died on November 3, 1926. Her husband, Frank Butler, died 18 days later. The couple had been married for 44 years. On Thanksgiving Day, 1926, they were buried alongside each other in Greenville, Ohio. Annie Oakley, the legend of "the Wild West," will always be remembered for her great sharpshooting skills.

Glossary

debt (DEHT) To owe other people money.

determination (dih-ter-meh-NAY-shun) The quality of being firm in purpose.

exaggerated (ihg-ZAH-juh-ray-ted) When a statement has been blown up beyond the truth to make it more interesting.

game (GAYM) The meat of wild animals that are hunted for food.

legend (LEH-jend) A story passed down through the years that many people believe.

markswoman (MARKS-wuh-mun) A woman who is skilled at shooting at a mark or target.

pony express (POH-nee ek-SPRESS) A system during 1860–61 that delivered letters across the western United States by riders on fast horses.

professional (pro-FEH-shuh-nul) A person who does something very well and is paid to do it.

prosperous (PRAHS-peh-rus) To be successful and wealthy.

Quakers (KWAY-kurz) People who follow a religion that believes in equality for all people, strong families, communities, and peace.

regiment (REH-jih-ment) A unit of soldiers.

sharpshooters (SHARP-shoo-terz) People who are skilled at shooting accurately.

Sioux (SOO) A Native American people from North America's plains.

stunts (STUNTZ) Acts that require special skills or strength.

symbol (SIM-bul) A person, object, or design that stands for something important.

Index

Web Sites

To learn more about Annie Oakley, check out these Web sites:
www.cowgirlsdream.com/bk_cowgirls.htm
www.dorchesterlibrary.org/library/aoakley.html
www.ormiston.com/annieoakley/films.html
www.ormiston.com/annieoakley/v.177.html